Your Ultimate Planning Guide & Workbook

BY NIKI RAKOWITZ

Published by She Rises Studios Publishing www.SheRisesStudios.com.

LIMITS OF LIABILITY/DISCLAIMER OF WARRANTY:

The author and publisher of this book have used their best efforts in preparing this material. While every attempt has been made to verify the information provided in this book, neither the author nor the publisher assumes any responsibility for any errors, omissions, or inaccuracies.

The author and publisher make no representation or warranties with respect to the accuracy, applicability, or completeness of the contents of this book. They disclaim any warranties (expressed or implied), merchantability, or for any purpose. The author and publisher shall in no event be held liable for any loss or other damages, including but not limited to special, incidental, consequential, or other damages.

ISBN: 978-1-960136-77-0

let's get to know each other...

I'm Niki, the visionary behind CARE Travel, a luxury destination wedding planning service dedicated to making dreams a reality. With over 25 years of experience, my team at CARE Travel has mastered the art of creating unforgettable travel experiences that last a lifetime.

congratulations!

Planning a wedding is one of the most magical chapters of life, and we're honored to have you consider us for your destination wedding planning needs! Our team works tirelessly to deliver a personalized experience that will reflect the beauty of your unique love story.

To better help couples looking to plan the destination wedding of their dreams, I've curated this comprehensive guide to walk you through every step of the process. Designed to provide you with all the necessary resources you'll need, this guide will take you from selecting the perfect location to designing the ideal floral arrangements.

This guide is an excellent resource even if you choose to do it yourself, this will give you a solid foundation of expectations to have a wonderful destination wedding. From all of us at CARE Travel, we would love to work with you and your partner to create an event that celebrates the love you share.

xo, Niki

the wedding planning workbook

As a pairing to this comprehensive guide, I'm excited to also offer you our extensive wedding planning workbook!

As you read through the guide, you'll find places where you might need to jot something down or need to plan for that particular section. That's where our workbook comes in! The Workbook is in the second half of this book for easy access.

It's full of easy-to-use worksheets that correlate directly to the topics discussed in this guide.

how to use the workbook

Consider it your tangible Pinterest board where you can jot down all your notes, dreams, visions, and inspiration for your perfect wedding event!

Table of Contents

INTRODUCTION

why a destination wedding?

When it comes to your wedding day, choosing a destination offers endless possibilities to create cherished memories that will stand the test of time. Because a destination wedding is not just about the destination itself; it's about making your wildest dreams come true.

imagine...

Picture yourself exchanging your vows in your dream vacation spot, surrounded by the views only that location could provide.

Whether you're envisioning an intimate elopement with only the closest family members or a grand celebration bringing everyone together, the possibilities are endless.

we can help!

If you and your partner are passionate about creating an extraordinary wedding, let us be your guide! At CARE Travel, we specialize in curating these unique and unforgettable moments that will leave a lasting impression on you and your guests.

Together, we'll work to make love, celebration, and adventure intertwine to create a truly unparalleled wedding experience.

the perks

You might be surprised to find out how reasonable a destination wedding can be! You can actually save up to 40% compared to traditional weddings.

Enjoy the ultimate trifecta—a wedding, honeymoon, and holiday, all in one! Once you bid farewell to your guests, you'll enjoy precious extra moments of honeymoon bliss with your partner!

Forget the single-day experience—with a destination wedding, your celebration can span an entire week, allowing you to truly immerse yourself in the joyous atmosphere.

Booking a certain number of guests at your chosen hotel or resort can score you exclusive perks such as a complimentary honeymoon suite!

Leave the worries of everyday life behind and fully immerse yourself in the magic of your wedding. Being in a foreign place allows you to forget about the stresses that accompany normal life.

A destination wedding provides the perfect opportunity to curate an intimate guest list. Limited availability of rooms at the resort allows you to prioritize the presence of those who truly matter to you.

PLANNING *process*

your roadmap

Whether you choose to partner with us or explore the world of destination weddings on your own, we're here to provide you with a comprehensive outline of what you can expect along the way!

select your dates

When planning a destination wedding, it is always recommended to begin the planning process at least 18 months in advance.

This not only helps ensure you have enough time, but also ensures you're getting the best rates and availability at your destination.

choose your destination & resort

Consider enlisting the expertise of a Destination Wedding Specialist—they'll be able to guide you toward the best destinations and resorts for your vision.

With their help, you can make your dream a reality without compromising on your budget.

secure resort reservation & room rates

Start enquiring about group contract rates for your date! This ensures that your guests are accounted for and have space in the resort of your choice.

Note that many resorts will require this reservation to be booked before they can confirm your wedding.

inform your guests!

It is highly recommended and common courtesy to allow your guests at least one year to prepare and start making initial deposits on travel and accommodations for your wedding.

Always encourage guests to make their deposits as soon as possible to reserve their space and preferred rate.

your roadmap

schedule your pre-travel consultation

At this first consultation, you'll likely receive a lengthy packet with a lot of information—don't panic! This is just for you to reference along the way.

I can also help you break it down into more bite-sized pieces and schedule a Zoom consultation with your coordinator three months prior to your departure date to ensure everything is running smoothly!

organize your planning timeline

While it may seem overwhelming at first, that's what this guide is for! Start organizing your basics to get ahead of the curve, and know that most resorts won't look at your details until three months prior to your date.

While this might seem late to you, I promise they have this down to a science!

break things down

We'll start by breaking the process up into bite-sized pieces, which makes the experience enjoyable instead of stressful.

Make sure to avoid trying to work too far ahead. Just take your time, and enjoy each step of this exciting process!

finalize & confirm

Around 30-45 days before your special day, we'll start confirming that all those elements are in place! Once everything is ready for review, be sure to schedule time with your coordinator to walk through everything TOGETHER—this will help avoid any miscommunication before your big day.

PLANNING *timeline*

PLANNING TIMELINE

let's do this!

18-24 MONTHS BEFORE

- [ ] Hire a travel planner
- [ ] Set a budget
- [ ] Start researching destinations
- [ ] Choose a date & ceremony style (legal, symbolic)
- [ ] Plan your site visit with a certified travel planner for discounts
- [ ] Start creating a guest list and collecting addresses
- [ ] Shop for wedding dresses!

12-18 MONTHS BEFORE

- [ ] Reserve your date & room block at resort
- [ ] Build a wedding website
- [ ] Mail out save the dates
- [ ] Review available wedding packages
- [ ] Research and book a photographer
- [ ] Choose and contact your bridal party
- [ ] Review passport expiration & apply for renewal

let's do this!

6-12 MONTHS BEFORE

- [ ] Define your dream wedding vision board
  Consider color scheme, ceremony location, flower type, events, food, and entertainment
- [ ] Create a wedding or honeymoon registry
- [ ] Shop for and decide on bridal party attire
- [ ] Select wedding day jewelry and accessories
- [ ] Finalize guest list and mail out invitations
- [ ] Create ceremony and reception playlist

3-6 MONTHS BEFORE

- [ ] Schedule wedding coordination consultation
  Discuss the location, vision and decor, menu selection, desired beauty and spa treatments
- [ ] Curate your bridal party gifts
- [ ] Plan and shop for welcome bags for guests
- [ ] Attend your final gown fitting
- [ ] Write your vows

let's do this!

1-2 MONTHS BEFORE

- ☐ Confirm your resort room reservations
- ☐ Confirm transportation to/from airport & resort
- ☐ Schedule final planning consultation with coordinator about 45 days prior to travel
- ☐ Confirm all event details with appropriate parties
- ☐ Create event itinerary for vendors & bridal party

2 WEEKS BEFORE

- ☐ Collect and review all travel documents—review with your travel planner
- ☐ Pack all wedding accessories
- ☐ Verify your flights and travel itinerary
- ☐ Walk through every step to catch any oversight
    - ☐ Collect pre-travel documents
    - ☐ Resort check-in time
    - ☐ Review any transfers
    - ☐ Work with your travel agent for full destination preparation

let's do this!

UPON ARRIVAL

- [ ] Conduct an on-site review with wedding coordinator
- [ ] Walk through the location(s) of your events
- [ ] Confirm all details for spa, food, and entertainment
- [ ] Request to have your dress and wedding attire steamed
- [ ] Assemble welcome gifts & leave with them reception or coordinator

YOUR WEDDING DAY!

- [ ] Ensure the ring bearer is prepared and has rings
- [ ] Coordinate with bridal party on duties and arrival time
- [ ] Arrive at the spa for hair and makeup
- [ ] Sit back with a glass of champagne and soak it all in!

DESTINATION WEDDING'S

quick checklist

PRE-PLANNING

- [ ] Create a dedicated email address for all wedding communications to keep things organized.
- [ ] Consider creating a wedding #hashtag so you and guests can share the experience on social media!

BOOKING

- [ ] Make your location and resort decision and make sure your wedding date deposit is confirmed with your venue.
- [ ] Your travel reservation has been booked, paid for, and confirmed.
- [ ] Your group rate contract or your group code has been signed and/or confirmed in writing by your chosen resort/venue.

NEXT STEPS

- [ ] Send out Save the Dates to all guests (complete this step only after all contracts are signed and your reservation is confirmed).
- [ ] Review the Wedding Packet from your resort and ensure it contains the contact information for your coordinator.
- [ ] Schedule your virtual planning consultation with the coordinator and be prepared to share your vision and walk through your options together.
- [ ] Make all final payments for rooms, contracts, and reservations.
- [ ] Schedule your final wedding virtual walk through and make the final payment to the resort/venue.

Q&A

frequently asked

questions?

You're not alone—I've had couples ask questions on just about everything!

Consider this guide your go-to resource and let my 25+ years of experience serve as your compass toward a seamless and magical wedding experience.

what are we expected to pay for?

the couple

the ceremony costs

reception: dinner & entertainment

bridal party hair & makeup

any group events guests are expected to participate in (excursions/tours)

private transfers for parents and/or grandparents

room upgrades for special guests

the guests

travel costs: flights, room stay, transfers, travel insurance

individual tours/excursions or spa treatments

any dinners on their own

drinks if you opt out of an open bar

is it possible to have a destination wedding under $10k?

Absolutely! There are a number of ways you can effectively manage the expense of your destination wedding. By adopting a simple or minimalistic approach to decor and staying flexible, many couples are able have the wedding of their dreams without sacrificing their budget.

In fact, here are a few examples to get you started!

*Please note that there are many variables that can affect cost, and these examples do not include travel costs.

Mexico

for $30k

95 guests

A complete wedding decor package with upgrades

A plated dinner, signature tequila drink, and a dessert cart

DJ entertainment for a full 3 hours

Jamaica

for $14k

32 guests

Upgraded floral package

A plated dinner, with a signature drink

DJ entertainment for a full 3 hours and a fireworks exit

St Lucia - Antigua

under $10k

16 guests

Upgraded floral package & arch

A buffet menu with a signature drink

DJ entertainment for a full 3 hours

who should we invite to our destination wedding?

This is your moment to shine, where every detail reflects your unique journey, including the guest list! Whether you envision an intimate gathering or grand celebration, the choice is entirely yours.

Know that guests typically bear their own travel expenses, so the size of your wedding doesn't have to greatly impact your budget.

In fact, some all-inclusive resorts will offer exclusive perks for booking additional rooms!

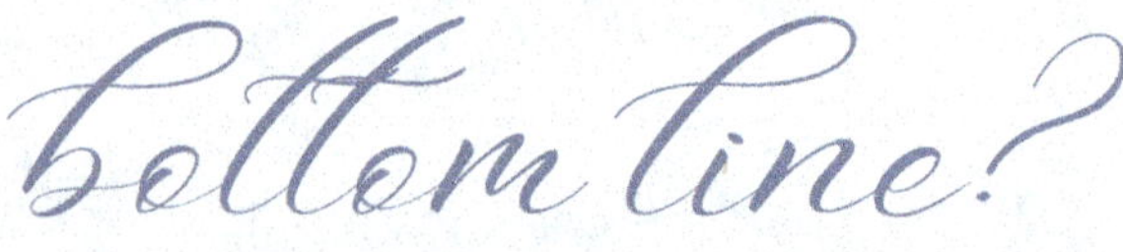

Embrace the freedom to curate a guest list that accompanies your vision and dreams. Select those that have had a special place in your journey and create an intimate atmosphere that reflects your individual love story!

This is your day—make sure you'll enjoy every second!

Find our worksheet to managing your guest list in the workbook!

what do I need to know about hiring a wedding travel agent?

The most important part of considering a wedding travel planner or agent is doing the research! I recommend interviewing one or two agencies to make sure you find the right match!

You'll want to find someone that aligns with your needs and meshes with your personalities, so maintaining transparent and open communication is key. Be honest with them about what you want, and even let them know you're exploring multiple agencies—being upfront is the best way to get the same in return.

- what do your services include?
- what costs and fees can we expect when hiring you?
- what would the booking process look like?
- what kind of relationship do you have with the resorts you recommend?
- what is your turnaround time for returning contracts?
- have you personally experienced the resorts you recommend?

IMPORTANT

Be wary of agencies claiming a contract confirmation within one week or less. Resorts take their time crafting and sending rates and proposals. Only then is this followed by formal contracts that require signing and deposits.

This is a big decision, and you don't need to feel pressured to compromise on things that are important to you! Don't be afraid to ask questions, and keep interviewing until you find the right fit for YOU.

Find our worksheet to interviewing travel advisors in the workbook!

what exactly does "all-inclusive" mean?

Great question! Unfortunately, there's no one size fits all answer when it comes to all-inclusive resorts. Some may include every detail you could imagine, while others only cover meals and drinks.

questions to ask...

these questions are a good way to start to compare various resorts and what is included in their "all-inclusive" pricing:

- what do you include in your "all-inclusive" plan?
- does it include transfers to and from the resort and airport?
- are there any additional costs at select dining locations?
- what brands of alcohol and soft drinks are available in this option?
- how often will our minibars be restocked?
- is tipping included in the price?
- are water sports included? if so, which ones?
- how far in advance can we make dining reservations?
- can we pre-book your spa services?

why do we have to pay for the reception dinner at an "all-inclusive" venue?

This is one of our most asked questions, and we get it, it seems confusing!

The best way we can explain this cost is what you are paying for the "private event" extras. These are things like the sole use of the location and the staffing that will be dedicated to your group exclusively for that amount of time.

Resorts require this additional fee because you won't be having your reception as a standard on-site dinner.

Resorts typically aren't staffed to take care of groups over six people at a time.

Additionally, larger groups tend to overwhelm the dining environment, therefore affecting other guests' experiences.

While many resorts will not allow you to have your reception dinner at an on-site restaurant as a whole group, there may be exceptions.

If you go this route, note the following:

- You will likely end up sitting apart and getting seated at different times.
- You'll face longer dinner times, close to two hours.

what is a group contract?

When selecting your resort or hotel for your destination wedding, they will likely request that you sign what is called a group contract. This is a signed agreement between you and the hotel that guarantees a certain number of rooms for your selected dates at set rates.

are there any perks to group contracts?

Yes! But perks may vary by the size of your group contract, your selected resort, and more, so make sure to ask what benefits they may offer!

Here are a few of the most common benefits for groups of 10 or more rooms:

Room Upgrade for the Couple
(based on availability)

Free Rooms (for example, for every 12 rooms, get 1 free)

This can be a great perk for you, as this perk is often earned as a "credit." Just know that it's usually based on the lowest category room for the shortest stay when being calculated the value of this “credit”.

Free Private Events (based on group size)
Typically, 10 rooms will earn a free hour-long private event, 20 rooms a two-hour-long event. These can be used for welcome cocktail parties, the rehearsal dinner, or even the reception dinner!

DATES
to remember

dates to remember

These dates will be important in keeping your guests up to speed on your event and making sure everyone's travel and accommodations are booked accordingly. Your travel dates, event date, and group contract dates will dictate the following:

- SAVE THE DATES ______________________

Plan to send Save the Dates out 12 months prior to your wedding date. You will want an RSVP deadline date as well, and we recommend setting this date around three weeks before your group block release date. This will ensure everyone who wants a room gets the rate you agreed upon!
TIP: If you have a travel advisor, they can handle RSVP reminders for you!

- DEPOSIT DUE DATE ______________________

Ideally, you'll want to set this date two weeks before the actual due date. This will make sure any procrastinators have a little extra flexibility—make sure to send a reminder to all guests a week before as a "last call!" (This is also something a travel advisor would handle for you!)

- FINAL PAYMENT DUE DATE ______________________

We also recommend setting this two weeks ahead of the true due date, and sending that one-week last call reminder. The more space you can give yourself for error, the better!

- GROUP CONTRACT
- ROOM RELEASE DATE ______________________

This is the final date you'll be able to release unused rooms from your contract without financial penalty. This date should correlate with your RSVP date, with RSVP's due three weeks prior to this.

- FLIGHT CONFIRMATIONS ______________________

If you are providing flights or other travel accommodations for any guests, make sure all confirmation notices are sent out at least 45 days prior to their travel.

- FINAL TRAVEL DOCUMENTS ______________________

All final travel documents and paperwork should begin arriving two weeks prior to your travel dates. We recommend viewing these in great detail for any discrepancies.

Find our worksheet to tracking your important dates in the workbook!

LET'S
break it down

the details

When the big picture starts to feel like too much, we break it down into the core pieces of the event! By organizing things this way, you can build smaller, more manageable to do lists to keep you moving in the right direction.

WELCOME COCKTAILS

REHEARSAL DINNER

THE CEREMONY

COCKTAIL HOUR

THE RECEPTION

ADDITIONAL OPTIONS

CREATING *your budget*

the investment

DESCRIPTION	COST ESTIMATE	QUANTITY	TOTAL
License/Govt. Fee	$150	N/A	$150
Location/Venue Fee	Included	up to 32	included
Officiant	Included in Venue Fee	N/A	$0
Photography Package	$4,000	N/A	$4,000
Cake (2 Tiers)	$300	up to 32	$300
Flowers & Decor	$3,000	N/A	$3,000
Hair & Makeup	$500	N/A	$500
Cocktail Party	Included	32	$0
Reception Dinner	$35/pp	32	$1,120
Reception Entertainment	$3000	3 hours	$3000
Reception Lights & Dance Floor	$3,000	3 hours	$3,000
Outside Vendor Fees	$1,000	N/A	$1,000

Average Grand Total of About $16,000

SUMMARY

TRAVEL AVERAGE	CEREMONY AVERAGE	RECEPTION AVERAGE
7 nights - $5,000	$6,000	$8,500

THINGS TO REMEMBER:

Many all-inclusive resorts:

- include the government fee in their packages
- offer garden, beach, and gazebo locations at no additional cost
- offer FREE wedding packages that include flowers and cake

We always recommend taking a photographer with you. The average cost is about the same, you'll get to know your photographer before you go, you'll get an extra room in your group numbers, and will avoid the outside vendor fee for photography in most cases.

Find our budget planning worksheets in workbook!

CHOOSING YOUR

destination

The list of incredible destination resorts and venues is endless—here's how you can start to narrow down your choices!

BUDGET FRIENDLY

Some of the most budget-friendly destinations include Mexico, Jamaica, and the Dominican Republic.

If you have slightly more wiggle room in your finances, consider St. Lucia, Antigua, Barbados, and Grenada for slightly more unique options!

OTHER FACTORS

- Decide ahead of time if you and your partner want children at your wedding, or if you prefer a kids-free event—this will help narrow down some of the resort choices.
- Skip "wedding mill" resorts. These resorts book multiple weddings in a single weekend. Instead, choose a resort that has a limit for each date.
- Know and understand that you won't be able to make everyone happy with your selection. Instead, choose your destination based on what works best for you and your partner and makes YOU happy.
- Do your research to understand what "all-inclusive" truly means for each resort you're considering. It doesn't always mean the same thing.
- Holidays might seem like an ideal date for your wedding, as guests will have time off to travel. However, this will also mean some of the highest rates and travel costs! Plan accordingly.
- Do not select your destination or resort solely based on another loved one's vacation experience—vacations are very different from weddings!

DEFINING *your vision*

your vision

From selecting the perfect color palette to crafting an ambiance that resonates with you and your love, this is your opportunity to shape every aspect of your day. Here's a sample of a vision planning board to get you started!

Find our board to plan your wedding vision in the workbook!

PLANNING *the main events*

welcome cocktails

Now, let's get to the fun part of planning—the main events!

We always recommend that our couples kick the wedding events off by hosting a welcome cocktail party!

Not only does this help couples get into the mood for the weekend, but it also helps the guests get to know family and friends they may not know!

What's the cost? A private cocktail event will typically be an additional charge ($12-19/person on average) and will include an open bar and a few hors d'oeuvres.

save some money by...

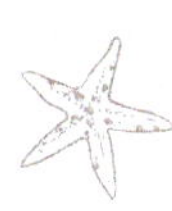

Keep it casual! Instead of reserving a private event, tell guests to plan on meeting at a bar for drinks together. We recommend outdoor locations for this option!

Use this as an opportunity to hand guests their welcome gifts and itineraries instead of having staff deliver them to each room!

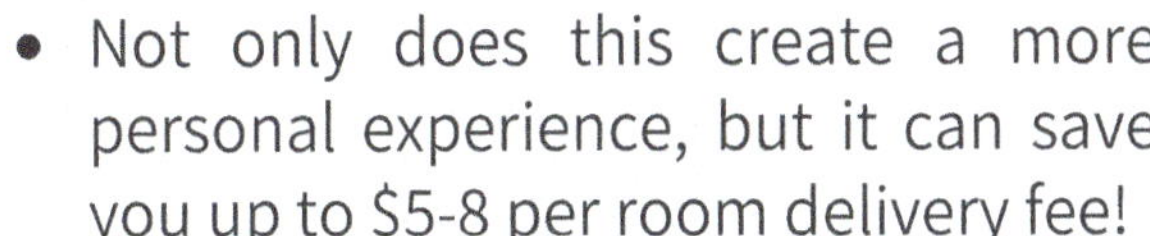

- Not only does this create a more personal experience, but it can save you up to $5-8 per room delivery fee!

Find our worksheet to planning your welcome cocktail vision board in workbook!

rehearsal dinner

Let's keep going, we still have more to plan...

Your rehearsal dinner will set the tone for your entire trip —by hosting your guests in a more casual setting, they'll be able to mingle and relax before the big day!

Remember that with a destination wedding, your guests will spend more time together than they would have in a more traditional wedding setting!

Having your rehearsal dinner at the start of the trip allows you to spend extra time with those you love and offers them the unique opportunity to truly get to know each other!

*An actual wedding rehearsal walk through can be set up with your on-site coordinator.

our top tips...

When selecting your time and location for the dinner, consider an early dinner such as 6 p.m. or a later dinner such as 8 p.m.

Keep your guest count close to 10 to be able to make a standard reservation instead of a private event!

If you prefer to host a larger, private event, you can expect a separate 3-5 course menu with slightly higher costs. ($15-30/person)

Note that most resort restaurants will not allow parties of 6 or more in without a reservation.

Find our worksheet to planning your rehearsal dinner vision board in workbook!

the ceremony

The ceremony features a lot of moving parts, so let's break it down in sections!

CEREMONY TYPE

Choosing the type of ceremony you want is a decision entirely up to you and your partner. The two main types of ceremonies are:

- Legal Ceremony
- Symbolic Ceremony—some destinations do not allow for symbolic ceremonies

If you elect to have a legal ceremony, make sure you know all the requirements your destination and resort may have.

TOP TIP: If your destination has strict legal ceremony requirements, have a local courthouse wedding to legalize the wedding ahead of time! None of your guests will be the wiser at your destination wedding!

THE VOWS

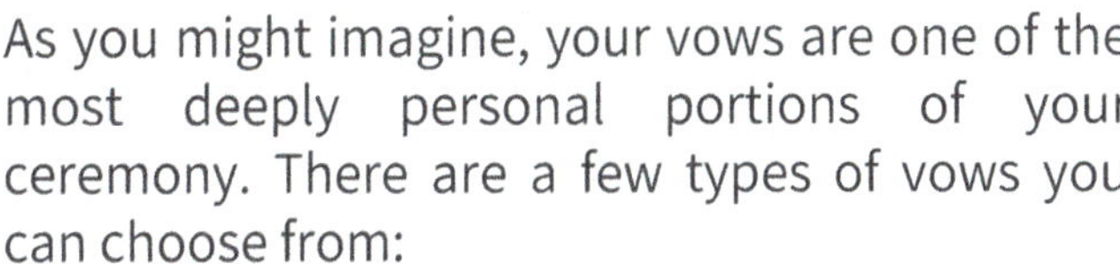

As you might imagine, your vows are one of the most deeply personal portions of your ceremony. There are a few types of vows you can choose from:

Standard/Traditional Vows
These are the vows most of us are familiar with seeing at weddings. These can be done in religious or non-religious formats.

Personally Written
These vows are when you and your partner elect to write your own personal vows.

Officiant
Whether you choose to hire your own officiant or use the one provided by your location, they can also assist in creating your vows!

Find our worksheets for creating a beautiful ceremony in workbook!

the ceremony

If you've selected an all inclusive resort destination, here are a few tips on what to expect and how to navigate having your ceremony on site!

REVIEW THE RESORT PACKAGES

Each resort likely has a number of wedding ceremony packages you can choose from. Make sure to review all of them to decide which package best suits your needs! Most all-inclusive resorts will even offer a free basic option that will come at no additional cost.

Note: You do not have to choose a package! If their standard packages do not speak to you, you're able to customize all components of your ceremony.

CHOOSE THE LOCATION

Carefully consider the location options your venue provides to find the location that works best for you and your guests! Resorts typically offer an array of location options, including gardens, beaches, piers, sky terraces, conference rooms, and more!

Note: Be prepared that sometimes a venue's most popular ceremony locations may come at an additional cost to reserve.

the ceremony

Here are a few other things you'll want to consider when planning your perfect ceremony!

THE FLORALS

- [ ] Bridal bouquet/boutonniere
  Expect average costs of $500 for bouquets, $40 for boutonnieres
- [ ] Parent's flowers (boutonnieres & wrist corsages)
- [ ] Bridal party (smaller bouquets & boutonnieres)
- [ ] Ring bearer and flower child (petals, boutonnieres)
- [ ] Altar/Arch/Gazebo florals
- [ ] Cocktail and Reception Centerpieces

THE PROCESSIONAL

This will be the order in which your parents, bridal party, and you will enter the ceremony! Here are a few things to consider:

- [ ] The Couple: Will you walk in on your own or with parents?
- [ ] The Parents: Consider the order you will have them walk in.
- [ ] Bridal Party: In what order will your party walk in? Who will they walk with?
- [ ] Children: Ring bearer, flower child
- [ ] Music: Will you have the same song for the full processional? Or different songs for each?
- [ ] The Bride: Who will she walk with? What song will be playing?

the ceremony

Here are a few other things you'll want to consider when planning your perfect ceremony!

THE DECOR

- ☐ **The Altar**
  Arch, gazebo, podium, or something different
- ☐ **Aisle or Walkway**
  Beach, wooden walkway, glass, or runner
- ☐ **Seats**
  Style, color, attached decor, layout
- ☐ **Lighting**
  Chandeliers, string lights, candles, etc

ANY ADD-ONS

NOTE: Upgrading the original packages may come with significant additional costs. Be sure to discuss your thoughts with your coordinator!

- ☐ Sand Ceremony
- ☐ Unity Ceremony
  Candle, Tie-Knot, Puzzle, Frame, etc
- ☐ Ring Warming
- ☐ Community Vows
- ☐ The Exit
  Confetti, bubbles, rice, sparklers, etc

cocktail hour

It's all about the details; be you, be unique.

The cocktail hour provides a little bit of a time buffer between your ceremony and seated dinner or reception. Couples use this time to take additional photos or just have a minute to enjoy being married!

Expect a private cocktail hour or party to come with some additional charges. The average cost is $12-19/person and typically comes with an open bar and three to five hors d'oeuvres options.

Some venues or resort group contracts may offer a one-hour cocktail party for your wedding as a group perk. This will vary depending on the number of guests and rooms booked.

your checklist

- ☐ Choose the Location & Time

  We recommend doing this immediately after the ceremony for about an hour!

- ☐ Select Your Menu

  Typically you'll choose 3-5 hors d'oeuvres. Remember to keep it light—dinner is next!

- ☐ Pick a Signature Drink

  A signature drink is a great way to control the alcohol served during cocktail hour!

  Consider creating a cute sign to advertise your signature drink.

Find our worksheet to planning your cocktail hour vision board in workbook!

the reception

The reception is likely one of the biggest parts of your day to plan! Here are a few things to consider as you get started.

THE SET UP

- ☐ Choose a time & location
  Typically directly after the cocktail hour, in a garden or banquet room
- ☐ Decide on the number of tables
  Most tables will seat 6-8 guests
- ☐ Style of Tables
  Typically round or rectangle
- ☐ Couples Seating
  Sweetheart table or with the rest of the bridal party?
- ☐ The Dessert Table

THE DINNER

- ☐ Dinner Style
  Typically plated or buffet style
- ☐ The Cake or Dessert
  Select style, flavor, and number of tiers
- ☐ The Bar
  Will you offer a full bar, select options, or signature drink only?
- ☐ Seating Chart
  Make sure to note any dietary restrictions or requirements when mapping your guests' seating.

Find our worksheets for planning the reception of your dreams in workbook!

the reception

Here are a few other things you'll want to consider when planning your perfect party to celebrate and let loose!

THE DECOR

- ☐ The Lighting
  Uplighting, candles, chandeliers, etc.
- ☐ Tabletop
  Tablecloths, runners, centerpieces, etc.
- ☐ Sweetheart/Bridal Party Table
  Flowers, lights, drapery
- ☐ Additional Signage
  Seating charts, hashtag use, large "LOVE" signs

ENTERTAINMENT

NOTE: Upgrading the original packages may come with significant additional costs. Be sure to discuss your thoughts with your coordinator!

- ☐ The DJ or Live Band
- ☐ Select Dances
  First Dance, Parents Dances, etc
- ☐ Song Choices
- ☐ The Dance Floor
- ☐ Fireworks
  First dance or at Exit

after-wedding brunch

The after-wedding brunch is certainly not a necessary activity, but is a relatively customary, nice touch! Consider it a quiet and intimate way to wrap up your wedding by recapping the fun everyone had!

BRUNCH DETAILS

A private brunch event can come with additional charges, so budget for an average of $12-19 per person! This will include a selected menu you can create, as well as some form of drink.

- ☐ Choose your location, time, and guest list for brunch

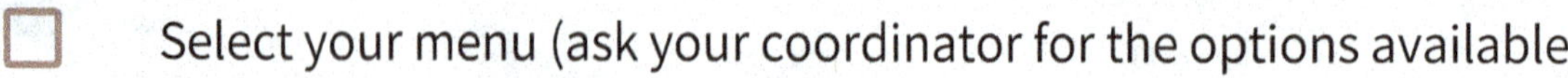

- ☐ Select your menu (ask your coordinator for the options available)

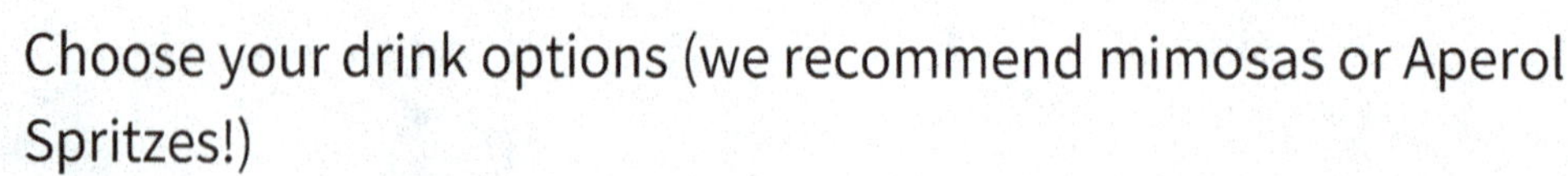

- ☐ Choose your drink options (we recommend mimosas or Aperol Spritzes!)

Find our worksheet to planning your after wedding brunch vision board in workbook!

CHOOSING
extras & add ons

spa services

There's no better time to truly pamper yourself than for your wedding! We always recommend using your wedding coordinator to book and confirm your services.

FAVORITE SERVICES

- [ ] Bridal Hair & Makeup

  This will include your trial and the day of.

- [ ] Couple's Massage

  Book the day after your arrival to relax and unwind from all the planning.

- [ ] Bridal Party Hair & Makeup

  Note if there are any restrictions to how many services can be booked for one time.

TIPS WHEN BOOKING

Hair and makeup can be provided in your room for an additional cost.

Your resort may offer a special bridal suite to get ready in with your wedding party at an additional cost.

Find our worksheet to planning your spa selections on page 40 of our wedding planning workbook!

music selection

Music plays a big role in any wedding and is a great way to personalize and add sentimental value to your event.

We always suggest sending your wedding coordinator your songs, artists, and a link to the exact version you want to avoid any confusion day of. Make sure to always save a copy for yourself to revisit!

what songs do you need?

CEREMONY

Processional
Parents & Bridal Party Entrance

Unity Ceremony

Recessional
Couple's Exit from Ceremony

Guest Exit
Select 3 songs

RECEPTION

First Dance
The Couple's First Dance Song

Specialty Dances
Parents' Dances, etc.

Do & Don't Play
Guidelines of songs the couple do and don't like

Last Song

Find our playlist planning worksheets in workbook!

group events

Group events are a great way to ensure that your guests have an exciting and enjoyable destination wedding experience! You can choose whether you'd like to take care of the bill for these events or not—it's entirely up to you and your budget!

You can let your guests know on the invitations or your wedding website about the events/excursions you're planning and make it clear if they will be "free" or additional costs for them! Use phrases like "Join us for a zip-lining adventure," or "Come for a boat ride with us," to imply that you are covering the cost. Be sure to include prices for each event you won't be covering.

EVENT IDEAS

- ☐ Scavenger Hunt

  Ask your coordinator for help organizing and selecting tasks!

- ☐ Bachelor/Bachelorette Party Bar Crawl

- ☐ Group Classes

  Some of our favorites include cigar rolling or sip & paint!

- ☐ Private Catamaran Rental

- ☐ Group Tours of Your Destination Location

Find our group events planning worksheets in workbook!

outside vendors

You may find that your selected location offers everything you need for your wedding day as resorts often have exclusive partnerships with local vendors. These vendors won't require you to pay a vendor fee because of that partnership!

However, if you find yourself in need of an additional vendor not provided by your location (DJ, photography, videography, decor, etc.), expect to pay an "outside vendor" fee of up to $1,000+ per vendor.

WAYS TO SAVE MONEY WHEN WORKING WITH VENDORS

If you're bringing a professional photographer along, consider covering three to four nights of their stay, and add them to your group block to avoid the outside vendor fee!

Select a reception location where you would not need to add a dance floor. Use that savings to invest more in the venue's recommended DJ—most resort-provided DJ services are excellent!

Save on decor vendors by bringing your own basic decor—think silk flowers for centerpieces, signage, and other small touches. (Make sure you have these approved by your coordinator ahead of time!)

Use those perks! The more rooms that book into your group block (like outside vendors!) will earn you more perks at your resort.

Find a contact sheet and shot list checklists in workbook!

resort reservations

Resort reservations are a great example of when having a travel professional on your side becomes necessary! These agents can keep track of your guest bookings, special requests, and travel needs.

Basically, they'll handle all your guests' needs so you don't have to! They can also ensure that your entire group is linked together, earning you those perks and amenities that come with group bookings!

GROUP ROOM RESERVATION DETAILS

When booking, make note of the number of rooms needed to earn your desired perks. This will be your goal number of rooms!

Create a guest and group booking spreadsheet to keep track of who has booked and who still needs to.

Ask about room upgrades when available for you and your partner and any special guests!

Keep your resort group room contract or group code handy—you'll need it when sending invitations or creating your wedding website!

Let the resort know as soon as possible if any of your room reservations have special needs or requests.

Ask about what transportation is available or required to get guests to and from the airport and resort. The resort may require your flight details in order to secure your transportation.

thank you!

You've officially made it through our wedding planning guide! I truly hope this guide helped make your dream wedding destination feel not only more attainable, but easier to manage!

Seeing our clients experience their magical events is why we continue to do what we do, year after year. From all of us at CARE Travel, THANK YOU for trusting us on this magical journey.

Are you ready to get started planning the event of a lifetime? Contact us today!

 (785) 537 - 8444

 Travel@CARETravel.com

 2757 Rory Road
Manhattan, KS, 66502

THE WORKBOOK
Destination Wedding
BY
NIKI RAKOWITZ

Table of

contents

Q&A FREQUENTLY ASKED

managing the guest list

Print these sheets for your wedding planning binder to keep all guest information in one place!

MANAGING YOUR *guest list*

NAME(S)

ADDRESS

RSVP YES ☐ NO ☐ # IN PARTY ____ BOOKED IN GROUP YES ☐ NO ☐

CONTACT INFO

NAME(S)

ADDRESS

RSVP YES ☐ NO ☐ # IN PARTY ____ BOOKED IN GROUP YES ☐ NO ☐

CONTACT INFO

NAME(S)

ADDRESS

RSVP YES ☐ NO ☐ # IN PARTY ____ BOOKED IN GROUP YES ☐ NO ☐

CONTACT INFO

Q&A FREQUENTLY ASKED
interview notes

Print these sheets for your travel planner interviews to keep notes on key points! I recommend interviewing three planners to ensure you find your best fit!

TRAVEL PLANNER

interviews

PLANNER

AGENCY/BUSINESS

WEBSITE

EMAIL

RATES (GROUP, SINGLE OCCUPANCY, DOUBLE OCCUPANCY

WHAT IS INCLUDED (FLIGHTS, INSURANCE, TRANSFERS, TOURS)

ADDITIONAL NOTES/PERSONAL THOUGHTS

DATES ____________________

GROUP ROOM BLOCK
dates tracker

dates to remember

ITEM	DATE	AMOUNT	PENALTY
DEPOSIT DUE DATE			
FINAL PAYMENT DUE DATE			
DATE FOR ROOM RELEASE			
WEDDING PACKAGE FINAL PAYMENT			

Room blocks are a great way for the couple to save time and money, as well as earn perks!

For example, if one of your guests decides to book with a secondary site to save an extra $40 on their room, they won't be added to your resort's numbers for the event. Because of this, the couple is then responsible for adding them to the events and paying for their items separately (their seat for the ceremony or plate for dinner), which can cost about $50 more, per person.

However, by booking into your group, they'll be automatically added to your numbers at no extra cost to you. Instead, they will count toward perks that may save you money!

CREATING A BUDGET

planning sheets

welcome cocktails

DESCRIPTION	COST ESTIMATE
LOCATION RENTAL	
LINENS RENTAL	
FLORALS / CENTERPIECES	
LIGHTING	
APPETIZERS	
SIGNATURE DRINKS	
OPEN BAR	
ENTERTAINMENT	

rehearsal dinner

DESCRIPTION	COST ESTIMATE
LOCATION RENTAL	
LINENS RENTAL	
FLORALS / CENTERPIECES	
LIGHTING	
FOOD - APPETIZERS	
FOOD - MAIN COURSE	
FOOD - DESSERT	
SIGNATURE DRINKS	
OPEN BAR	

the ceremony

DESCRIPTION	COST ESTIMATE
LOCATION RENTAL	
ACTUAL CEREMONY COST	
FLORALS - BRIDAL BOUQUET	
FLORALS - BRIDAL PARTY BOUQUETS & BOUTONNIERE	
FLORALS - PARENT BOUTONNIERES	
FLORALS - CEREMONY ARCH	
DECOR - CHAIR BOWS/DRAPING	
DECOR - AISLE RUNNER/FLORALS	
DECOR - ENTRY SIGN & TABLE, GUEST BOOK	
CEREMONY ADD ONS (SPECIAL VOWS OR READINGS, UNITY CEREMONY, ETC)	
OFFICIANT	

cocktail hour

DESCRIPTION	COST ESTIMATE
LOCATION RENTAL	
LINENS RENTAL	
FLORALS / CENTERPIECES	
LIGHTING	
DECOR - SIGNAGE	
DECOR - PHOTO BACKDROPS	
APPETIZERS	
SIGNATURE DRINKS	
OPEN BAR	
ENTERTAINMENT	

the reception

DESCRIPTION	COST ESTIMATE
LOCATION RENTAL	
ENTERTAINMENT	
DANCE FLOOR	
DANCE FLOOR LIGHTING	
EXIT FIREWORKS	
DECOR - TABLECLOTHS	
DECOR - FLORALS & CENTERPIECES	
DECOR - ADDITIONAL LIGHTING	
PHOTOBOOTH OR WALL	
DECOR - SIGNAGE	
SPECIALTY ADD ONS (CHURRO CART, CHAMPAGNE WALL, FOOD TRUCK, ETC)	

after wedding brunch

DESCRIPTION	COST ESTIMATE
LOCATION RENTAL/RESERVATION	
LINENS RENTAL	
FLORALS / CENTERPIECES	
DECOR - SIGNAGE	
MENU SELECTIONS	
DRINK SELECTIONS	
GIFTS	
ENTERTAINMENT (IF DESIRED)	

NOTE: While an after-wedding brunch is never expected or required, it is often greatly appreciated by your closest guests!

DEFINING YOUR VISION

planning board

to get you started...

SAMPLE VISION

to get you started...

DEFINING

your overall vision

From selecting the perfect color palette to crafting an ambiance that resonates with you and your love, this is your opportunity to shape every aspect of your day.

COLOR PALETTE

PLANNING THE MAIN EVENTS

welcome cocktails

welcome cocktails

THE LOCATION

THE GIFTS

THE VIBE

THE DECOR

THE MENU

PLANNING THE MAIN EVENTS

rehearsal dinner

rehearsal dinner

THE LOCATION

THE VIBE

THE DECOR

THE MENU

EXTRA DETAILS

PLANNING THE MAIN EVENTS

the ceremony

YOUR VISION

the ceremony

THE LOCATION

THE VIBE

THE DECOR

THE FLOWERS

EXTRA DETAILS

seating chart

Here are a few other things you'll want to consider when planning your perfect ceremony!

CEREMONY SEATING

LEFT HAND SIDE		RIGHT HAND SIDE	
1	1	1	1
2	2	2	2
3	3	3	3
4	4	4	4
5	5	5	5
6	6	6	6
7	7	7	7
8	8	8	8
9	9	9	9
10	10	10	10

the processional order

01.	OFFICIANT
02.	PARENTS OF THE GROOM
03.	MOTHER OF THE BRIDE
04.	GRANDPARENTS
05.	THE GROOM
06.	BRIDESMAID + GROOMSMAN
07.	BRIDESMAID + GROOMSMAN
08.	BRIDESMAID + GROOMSMAN
09.	RING BEARER + FLOWER GIRL
10.	BRIDE + HER ESCORT

For the Processional Playlist planning sheet, skip to page 35 in the Music Planning section.

the recessional order

01. BRIDE + GROOM

02. FLOWER GIRL + RING BEARER

03. BRIDESMAID + GROOMSMAN

04. BRIDESMAID + GROOMSMAN

05. BRIDESMAID + GROOMSMAN

06. PARENTS OF THE BRIDE

07. PARENTS OF THE GROOM

08. GRANDPARENTS

09. OFFICIANT

For the Recessional Playlist planning sheet, skip to page 36 in the Music Planning section.

PLANNING THE MAIN EVENTS

cocktail hour

YOUR VISION

cocktail hour

THE LOCATION

THE GIFTS

THE DECOR

THE VIBE

THE MENU

PLANNING THE MAIN EVENTS

the reception

YOUR VISION

the reception

THE LOCATION

THE VIBE

THE DECOR

THE FLOWERS

THE MENU

seating chart

RECEPTION SEATING CHART

TABLE ONE		TABLE TWO		TABLE THREE	
1	4	1	4	1	4
2	5	2	5	2	5
3	6	3	6	3	6

TABLE FOUR		TABLE FIVE		TABLE SIX	
1	4	1	4	1	4
2	5	2	5	2	5
3	6	3	6	3	6

menu planning

APPETIZER

MAIN COURSE

DESSERT

the grand exit

TIMING

THE MUSIC

TRANSPORTATION

THE VIBE

THE EXTRAS
Fireworks, sparklers, bubbles, etc

PLANNING THE MAIN EVENTS

after-wedding brunch

YOUR VISION

after-wedding brunch

THE LOCATION

THE VIBE

THE DECOR

THE GUEST LIST

THE MENU

EXTRAS & ADD ONS
spa services

spa services

DESCRIPTION	COST ESTIMATE
BRIDE'S HAIR & MAKEUP	
BRIDAL PARTY HAIR & MAKEUP	
COUPLE'S MASSAGE	
BRIDAL SUITE RENTAL	
SERVICES IN SPA VS ROOM	
MANICURES/PEDICURES	
OTHER EVENT HAIR & MAKEUP	
FACIALS	
BRIDESMAID SPA OPTIONS	
WAXING	
EXTENSIONS - LASHES, HAIR, ETC	

EXTRAS & ADD ONS

music selections

THE MUSIC

the ceremony playlist

PROCESSIONAL

PARENTS / GRANDPARENTS ENTRANCE

THE GROOM

BRIDAL PARTY ENTRANCE

FLOWER GIRL/RING BEARER

THE BRIDE

THE MUSIC

the ceremony playlist

RECESSIONAL

THE COUPLE

BEST MAN & MAID/MATRON OF HONOR

THE BRIDAL PARTY

PARENTS OF THE COUPLE

GRANDPARENTS OF THE COUPLE

THE MUSIC

the ceremony playlist

OTHER SONGS

GUESTS ARE BEING SEATED

ANNOUNCEMENTS TO BE MADE

ANY ADDITIONAL SONGS DESIRED

the reception playlist

BRIDAL PARTY ENTRANCE

COUPLE'S ENTRANCE

IMPORTANT ANNOUNCEMENTS

COUPLE'S FIRST DANCE

FATHER/DAUGHTER DANCE

MOTHER/SON DANCE

the reception playlist

CAKE CUTTING

SPECIAL GUESTS' SONGS

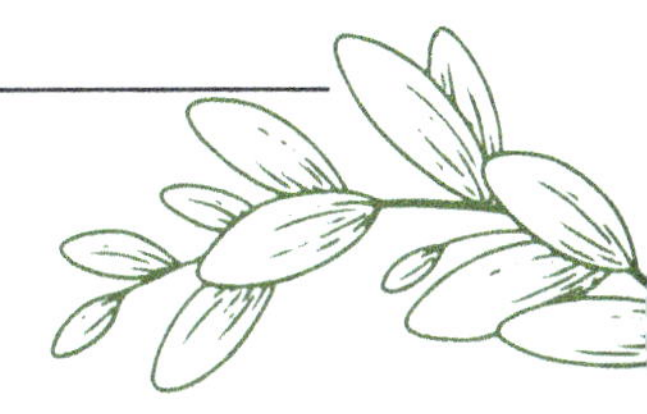

LAST DANCE SONG

ADDITIONAL SPECIALTY SONGS

EXTRAS & ADD ONS

group events

group events

DESCRIPTION - IDEAS	COST ESTIMATE

EXTRAS & ADD ONS
outside vendors

contact sheet

VENDOR	NAME	CONTACT	NOTES
Day-of Coordinator			
Venue Coordinator			
Officiant			
Florist			
Decorator			
Photographer			
Videographer			
DJ / Band			
Makeup Artist			
Hair Stylist			
Cake			
Photobooth			

- [ ] Bride & Groom with all Parents
- [ ] Bride & Groom with both Immediate Families
- [ ] Bride & Groom with Groom's Parents
- [ ] Bride & Groom with Bride's Parents
- [ ] Bride & Groom with Groom's Mother
- [ ] Bride & Groom with Groom's Father
- [ ] Bride & Groom with Groom's Siblings
- [ ] Bride & Groom with Bride's Mother
- [ ] Bride & Groom with Bride's Father
- [ ] Bride & Groom with Bride's Siblings
- [ ] Bride with Both Parents
- [ ] Bride with Mother
- [ ] Bride with Father
- [ ] Bride with Siblings
- [ ] Bride with Grandparents
- [ ] Groom with Both Parents
- [ ] Groom with Mother
- [ ] Groom with Father
- [ ] Groom with Siblings
- [ ] Groom with Grandparents

OTHER SHOTS:

the details

- [ ] Invitation Suite
- [ ] Entrance / Welcome Sign
- [ ] Guest Book
- [ ] Aisle Florals & Chair Decor
- [ ] Full Ceremony Set Up
- [ ] Basket or Display of Essentials (sunglasses, sunscreen, fans, heel protectors, etc)
- [ ] Musicians
- [ ] Cocktail Hour Space without Guests
- [ ] Cocktail Hour Space with Guests
- [ ] Bar Floral Arrangements
- [ ] Bar Decor (custom napkins, drink stirrers, signage, signature drink, etc)
- [ ] Bar Floral Arrangements

OTHER SHOTS:

the bride

- [ ] Veil Over Head
- [ ] Putting on Earrings/Jewelry
- [ ] Holding Glass of Champagne
- [ ] Looking Out the Window
- [ ] Walking with Bouquet
- [ ] Fixing Hair / Makeup
- [ ] Looking in the Mirror
- [ ] Putting on Shoes
- [ ] Looking Back at the Camera
- [ ] Popping Bottle of Champagne
- [ ] Photo in Bridal Pajamas

OTHER SHOTS:

the groom

OTHER SHOTS:

- [ ] Toasting with Groomsmen
- [ ] Flat Lay of Ring, Bow Tie, Cufflinks, Watch, Cologne, and Shoes
- [ ] Adjusting Bow Tie
- [ ] Adjusting Cufflinks
- [ ] Close Up of Cufflinks
- [ ] Holding a Drink
- [ ] Looking in the Mirror
- [ ] Close Up of Custom Suit/Embroidery
- [ ] Looking Out the Window
- [ ] Close Up of Watch

- [ ] Bridesmaids Opening Gifts
- [ ] Flat Lay of the Bridesmaid Gifts
- [ ] Bridal Party in their Pajamas
- [ ] Bride in Pajamas with Champagne
- [ ] Bride Applying Lipstick/Gloss in the Mirror
- [ ] Bridal Party Toasting with Champagne
- [ ] Close up of Champagne Cheers
- [ ] Bride Having Her Makeup Applied
- [ ] Bride Fixing Her Hanging Dress
- [ ] Pajamas or Dresses on Custom Hangers
- [ ] Bride's Perfume Bottle
- [ ] Wedding Gown Hanging
- [ ] Wedding Shoes
- [ ] Wedding Jewelry
- [ ] Reception Dress
- [ ] Row of Shoes

OTHER SHOTS:

____

____

____

____

____

the ceremony

- [ ] Full Room Shot
- [ ] Wedding Party Walking Down the Aisle (Group & Individual)
- [ ] Bride Walking Down the Aisle
- [ ] Groom's First Look
- [ ] The Vows - Bride & Groom
- [ ] Unity Ceremony
- [ ] Exchanging of Rings
- [ ] The First Kiss as Mr. & Mrs.
- [ ] Couple Walking Down the Aisle
- [ ] Bridal Party Recession

OTHER SHOTS:

the reception

- [ ] Full Room Shot
- [ ] Close up of Centerpieces
- [ ] Wedding Party Entrance
- [ ] Bride & Groom Entrance
- [ ] The Toasts
- [ ] First Dance
- [ ] Mother/Son Dance
- [ ] Father/Daughter Dance
- [ ] Cake Cutting
- [ ] Bouquet / Garter Toss
- [ ] Dance Floor
- [ ] Grand Exit

OTHER SHOTS:

EXTRA *planning sheets*

tiktok ideas

GETTING READY	GOING TO THE CHAPEL
WHEN TO FILM:	WHEN TO FILM:
SHOTS REQUIRED:	SHOTS REQUIRED:
AUDIO:	AUDIO:
PEOPLE NEEDED:	PEOPLE NEEDED:
INSPO TIKTOKS	INSPO TIKTOKS

tiktok ideas

GETTING READY	GOING TO THE CHAPEL
WHEN TO FILM:	WHEN TO FILM:
SHOTS REQUIRED:	SHOTS REQUIRED:
AUDIO:	AUDIO:
PEOPLE NEEDED:	PEOPLE NEEDED:
INSPO TIKTOKS	INSPO TIKTOKS

packing lists

THE BRIDESMAIDS

- ☐ Bridesmaid Dress
- ☐ Shoes
- ☐ Jewelry
- ☐ Hair Tools
- ☐ Makeup Bag
- ☐ Clutch or Other Bag
- ☐ Wallet with ID & Hotel Key
- ☐ Bra, Shapewear, Undies
- ☐ Hair/Makeup Inspo Pics
- ☐ Hair Accessories
- ☐ Perfume
- ☐ Any Special Accessories

EMERGENCY KIT

- ☐ Advil/Tylenol
- ☐ Eyedrops
- ☐ Tums/Pepto
- ☐ Blister Bandaids
- ☐ Hand Sanitizer
- ☐ Bug Spray/Sunscreen
- ☐ Liners/Pads/Tampons
- ☐ Dental Floss
- ☐ Deodorant
- ☐ Razor
- ☐ Safety Pins
- ☐ Mints and Mouthwash
- ☐ Fashion Tape
- ☐ Tissues
- ☐ Sewing Kit
- ☐ Lint Roller

packing lists

THE GROOMSMEN

- [ ] Tux or Suit
- [ ] Tie
- [ ] Shoes
- [ ] Socks
- [ ] Cuff Links
- [ ] Comb and Hair Gel
- [ ] Wallet with ID & Hotel Key
- [ ] Cologne
- [ ] Undershirt/Underwear
- [ ] Belt
- [ ] Pocket Square
- [ ] Any Special Accessories

EMERGENCY KIT

- [ ] Advil/Tylenol
- [ ] Eyedrops
- [ ] Tums/Pepto
- [ ] Tide To Go
- [ ] Hand Sanitizer
- [ ] Bug Spray/Sunscreen
- [ ] Shoe Shine
- [ ] Dental Floss
- [ ] Deodorant
- [ ] Razor
- [ ] Extra Black Socks
- [ ] Mints and Mouthwash
- [ ] Nail Clippers
- [ ] Phone Charger
- [ ] Sewing Kit
- [ ] Lint Roller

thank you!

Congratulations on making it through the wedding planning workbook! I hope these pages helped you organize your planning process and take notes about any next steps on creating your perfect destination event!

Seeing my clients experience their magical events is why I continue to do what I do, year after year. THANK YOU for trusting me on this magical journey.

If you are interested in the services of a certified Destination Wedding Planner, the CARE Travel Team is here for you!
Contact us today to schedule your appointment!

 Travel@CARETravel.com

 https://caretravel.com

xo, Niki

www.ingramcontent.com/pod-product-compliance
Lightning Source LLC
Chambersburg PA
CBHW080422030426
42335CB00020B/2550

* 9 7 8 1 9 6 0 1 3 6 7 7 0 *